Shiva Jnana

RAJ BHAMBU

ANSHU CHAUDHARY

NOTION PRESS

Published by Notion Press 2023

India. Singapore. Malaysia.

Copyright © Raj Bhambu & Anshu Chaudhary 2023

ISBN: 979-8890671042

Dedicated to

The Graceful Almighty Bhagwan Shiva and

our loving father (Late) Sh. Shrichand Chaudhary

Contents

Acknowledgments vii

Introduction ix

Invocations to the Almighty Shiva 1

1. The Beginning 3

2. The Brahman 13

3. Consciousness.. 23

4. Knowledge 27

5. Apparent Duality... 31

6. The Self 43

7. Glories of Mahadeva 51

8. Sacred texts 61

9. The Seeker 71

10. Self-realization... 81

11. Spiritual path 89

Epilogue 97

About Authors 98

Acknowledgments

This humble attempt has been possible with the blessings of Realized souls such as Sri Ramana Maharishi, Sri Nisargdatt Maharaj, Baba Bujan Nath, and numerous others; and literature of enlightened *jnanis* such as Swami Chinamayanand and Swami Vivekananda.

In personal life, deeper dive into the spiritual realm was the result of the void that we felt due to sudden dehavasan of our father Sh. Shrichand Chaudhary, who left the earthly realm all of a sudden and we felt like a dry leaf in a storm. However, his grace, blessings and a constant subtle presence in our lives brought strength and guided us on this path. We shall always be indebted to him for the same, apart from everything that he has been doing for us over several lives, in every form.

Our first brush with spirituality was owing to our grandparents, who always did japa of the formless Almighty during daily *Snan* i.e. ablutions.

Lastly, our mother's eternal love, blessings, encouragement and support has withstood us at every step of our life and she has been a patient witness and a great motivator during writing of this book, showering her blessings.

Introduction

'*Shiva Jnana*' is based on the cryptic and sacred aphorisms and slokas through which Lord Shiva had taught *atma-vidya* to sage Ribhu. These slokas and aphorisms are contained in the sixth *Adhyaya* (chapter) of *Sri Shiva Rahasya* and these have been narrated by Lord Skanda to sage Jagshaivya.

Skanda is the eldest son of Bhagwan Shiva and is also known by the names such as *Kartikeya, Subrahmanya, Shanmukha, Kumara and Murugan.*

Sage Ribhu, son of Lord Brahma, devoted himself to Lord Shiva single-mindedly and wished to attain '*atma-vidya*' from Bhagwan Shiva.

Pleased with his single-minded devotion, bhakti and selfless invocations, Lord Shiva taught *atma-vidya* i.e. knowledge of the 'Self' to sage Ribhu. Lord Skanda has attributed 146 slokas directly to Bhagwan Shiva in this sacred scripture.

This knowledge, bestowed by Bhagwan Shiva through these slokas to sage Ribhu, was later taught and explained in detail by sage Ribhu to his spiritually ripe disciple Nidagha (son of Maharshi Pulastya) and several other sages at Mount Kedara. This dialogue between sage Ribhu and Nidagha is referred to as the Ribhu Geeta.

'*Shiva Jnana*' is based on 146 slokas of the sixth *Adhyaya* of the *Sri Shiva Rahasya,* which are attributed directly to Bhagwan Shiva. It is neither exact translation nor transliteration of those slokas but is the essence of what Lord Shiva taught in those slokas.

The Almighty Shiva has succinctly described the creation of the universe, the Brahman, the Consciousness, the Self, apparent duality and the reasons thereof, role and import of the sacred texts, and Self-Realization and obstacles thereof.

'*Shiva Jnana*' will help every seeker in finding answers to the most basic questions of life and motivate him/her to delve deeper into the spiritual realm.

~ Om Namah Shivay ~

Invocations to the Almighty Shiva

Once we idolise someone and need his blessings, we generally sing praises of him, eulogise, glorify and applaud him, celebrate his every aspect or deed, extol and dignify him, honour and hero-worship him.

However, if someone needs blessings from the Almighty Shiva himself, then the glorification is a way of paying his/her obeisance and reverence, which comes straight from the heart, laden with emotion and is always full of love, honour, respect, devotion, faith and bhakti.

Before writing or reading this book, which explains the Instructions of Lord Shiva Himself, let us all pay our obeisance and reverence to the Almighty through a few lines of eulogies and praises of the omniscient, omnipresent, and omnipotent, and the absolute Bhagwan Shiva.

Blessed are those who think, read, write, reflect, contemplate and abide in the Almighty Shiva.

O Parmesvara, you are the Adi (beginning), the anta (end) and the Anant (eternal). There is nothing beyond you. You are beyond the beyond. You are the father, the mother, the siblings, the relatives, the friends, and the whole world for me.

You are the source and the supply of compassion and You always protect those who seek refuge in Your lotus feet and who always contemplate on You and Your mercy. You are the one resplendent like the bright sun.

O Lord Shiva, there is no end to Your glories and it is any seeker's great fortune that he acquires deep desire and devotion for union with 'You, the Almighty' and contemplates and meditates with You as the sole lakshay i.e. aim.

One who does so is certain to be bestowed Your protection and the Jnana (knowledge) which removes the avidya / ajnana (ignorance), thereby helping transcend the transmigratory cycles of rebirth.

O Shambhu, allow my mind to rejoice with identifying with You and let this universe be filled with the holy dust of Your auspicious feet.

O Bhagwan Shiva, the Almighty, kindly impart me the atma-vidya (Knowledge of the Self), the rare and true knowledge which stops rebirth cycles, ensures liberation and union with the 'Self'.

~ Om Namah Shivay ~

1. The Beginning

This chapter contain instructions by *Mahadevadideva Parmesvara Bhagwan Shiva* on the process of beginning of the each celestial time period, the reasons of creation and the worldly life and liberation.

Bhagwan Shiva proclaimed thus:

> ➤ Each *Yuga* (celestial time period) has several *manavantara* cycles. Upon the start of each such cycle, *Vyasas* manifest in several forms / bodies for the attainment and propagation of My knowledge (i.e. knowledge of Shiva, the ultimate and complete knowledge).

Vyasas are the partial incarnations of the Almighty who compile mantras of the Vedas and compiled or divided the Vedas into separate categories. Commonly, Vedavyasa is referred to as Vyasa, however, Swami Vivekananda opined that Vyasas may not have been single person but a lineage of sages who compiled sacred texts, without claiming authorship.

> ➤ These *Vyasas* put *bhasma* on their bodies, wear *rudraksh malas* and surrender their heart and soul entirely at My feet. Through these noble acts, they plunder my heart and

become worthy recipients of the ultimate knowledge.

➢ These precious teachings bring paramount wisdom and using this wisdom and rationale through acute self-discipline and guileless love to me, the *Vyasas* expound this knowledge and never contradict the *Vedic sutras*, precepts or principles.

➢ *'Brahma Sutras'* start with the word *'atha'*, which implies that the only *'subject'* worth knowing is *'Brahman' (pronounced as Brhmn).*

➢ This knowledge of Brahman can be attained by means of *Yoga, Jnana, Samkhya and the Upanishads* expounding the codes of *Atma-sanyam* (self-restraint), *pranayama* (breathing exercises), *Vivek* (discrimination between real and unreal), *atma-vishleshan* (self-analysis) and *atma-vichar* (self-enquiry).

➢ The adjuncts and qualities which are generally attributed to the illusory Reality such as names and forms are not to be used.

The illusory reality being referred to here is the world consisting of animate and inanimate forms which is comprehended by body, mind and intellect.

➢ The true knowledge of the 'Self' transcends names and forms and is to be lived at every moment of one's life, which results in effortless, natural, permanent and blissful experience of the knowledge of one's own 'Being'.

> To understand that the world is unreal, one must understand the reality of the world by enquiring into the principles expounded by *Brahma Sutras*.

> The universe has appeared by 'manifestation' of the supreme Brahman and it is not the *parinam* (result) of some physical phenomenon, as is generally believed.

It is generally believed that the creation of the world is a physical phenomenon wherein one event leads to another, thereby implying a cause-effect basis of the creation. However, that is not the case as per Shiva's instructions on the subject of creation of universe.

> With the help and guidance of scriptural utterances and one's own intellect, the truth will shine on you that Shiva alone is the cause behind this manifestation.

However, this (shining of truth) happens only with the Grace of the Almighty and a seeker cannot take it as a right and can neither fix a timeline for the same.

Mahesvara, the supreme Lord, is the supreme causeless cause of everything.

One may wonder – why new creation?

This is one question which always comes to the mind of every individual jiva during life in this world full of sorrow and pain as well as joy and pleasures.

It has been answered thus by Lord Shiva, which was narrated by Skanda:

Shiva is compassion embodied and He designs a new round of creation so that jivas can exhaust their accumulated *vasanas* (desires) and evolve spiritually.

Spiritual evolvement is possible only after exhaustion of accumulated *vasanas* and non-formation of new *vasanas*.

Though He, the Almighty Shiva, is bound by no such duty, yet He does so because of His compassion for His children, the *jivas*, their upliftment and evolvement.

Jivas get bodies and nature based on their past karmas, acquire their individuality (which they falsely consider existence) and then undergo growth, changes and evolution during their lifetime and perish in the end.

This explains the why i.e. the reason of any individual jiva's life on the earthly plane. Here growth, changes and evolution are those pertaining to spiritual evolvement and not physical one because physical body, mind, intellect and related faculties are just a means or vehicle and perish in the end, thereby leaving the spiritual evolvement as the only continuous aspect.

Thus, their hard-earned and proudly flaunted personalities dissolve in a moment. On the other hand, *Isvara*, the Almighty, exists without the aid of any body i.e. body or no body, He IS!

With His basic nature of *sat-chit-ananda* (Being-Knowledge-Bliss) and with no other adjuncts or qualities, He inspires and elevates jivas unto Himself.

It is usual that one always gets inspired by higher ones and since the basic nature of the Almighty is higher than jivas, it is natural for them to get inspired by the nature of Almighty and try to emulate it and be like Him. This is what is called spiritual evolvement.

He guides them through their false and transient personalities, relative and illusory knowledge of material sciences and sensual and pain-generating worldly enjoyments.

In this effort to uplift His children, the *jivas*, His patience is beyond any description and explanation.

Even if a *jiva* takes hundreds of thousands of birth for spiritual evolvement, Isvara is constantly with him during this journey, guiding him at every step, yet giving freedom to the jiva to choose one's own journey and pace.

Mahesvara, the almighty and His utterances, the Vedas, guide and direct each of the divergent jivas existing in the universe towards their common goal. Those who follow them reverentially receive His grace.

Those who are discharged with studying Vedas must do so with complete trust, devotion and reverence, under the guidance of pure and able Guru.

Further, they must propagate the teachings in their complete purity to the masses, for spiritual upliftment of the society, as a whole.

Worldly Life and Liberation

Even if one keeps progressing forward in the spiritual journey, one isn't free of the worldly pains, sorrows, enticements, desires etc. until Liberation from the triad of body, mind and intellect is achieved.

For achieving this Liberation, one needs to constantly practice vigilance, forbearance and self-enquiry.

One must discharge one's worldly duties with reverence and humility till in parallel with one's spiritual practices.

Thus, the false notion, that one needs to be a forest-dwelling ascetic for liberation, is clarified by the Almighty Himself.

It is more important to discharge one's duties in parallel with one's spiritual practices.

Thus, one exhausts past karmas and ensures that no new karmas are added. Once the causal force of *karma* gets exhausted, it lets the seeker free to march ahead on the *Jnana* (knowledge) path.

If a seeker's karma gets exhausted prior to attainment of *siddhi*, it is helpful in the attainment of the final goal.

However, if a seeker renounces the worldly duties prior to exhaustion of his *karma cycle*, then it adversely affects his spiritual journey, as such temporary relief from worldly duties creates more fear, doubt and agitations in mind, thereby creating more *karmas*.

Vairagya (renunciation) is not at all about renouncing worldly life but it is living worldly life and yet being constantly aware of the real (the Self) and unreal (world) and remaining completely detached while carrying-out one's duties.

A seeker must carry-out duties as laid down in the Smrities and if they are beyond one's capacity, then he should silently try his best but should never indulge in criticizing or doubting the sacred utterances.

The *karma* principle and its application in the life of jivas in this world has never been easy for the seekers and they have been often tried and tested in varying ways.

However, sincerity and perseverance has often been rewarded here in this world and beyond.

The sacred scriptures are meant to guide people of all strata and intellect and the symbol varies according to their spiritual capacities. Yet, all of them point unanimously to the non-dual Brahman.

The deities and gods (of common masses) with gross forms gradually reduce to subtle mystic words i.e. mantras of the educated to subtle mystic syllables i.e. *bijaksharas* of the sages or ripe seekers.

All these i.e. idol-worshipping common masses, mantra-chanting educated, and sages are on the spiritual journey at various stages and none of them need to be judged upon or compared.

All these ultimately lose all their qualities and attributes and subside or resolve into the transcendental Brahman.

The wise seekers recognize it early that worship of any form or name has no other goal or aim than the pure, non-dual Brahman.

Sandhya is the period when Mahadeva, the Almighty, withdraws his effulgence, radiance or light of the lights that illumine the universe and then all beings rest in him in abeyance with their tendencies remaining latent or dormant.

This is the period between dissolution of one creation and a fresh creation. This is how cosmic cycles work.

Thus, Lord Shiva succinctly described how new creation is done, why new creation takes place and what is the purpose of each individual being a part of that creation process.

~ *Om Namah Shivay* ~

2. The Brahman

This chapter elaborates on the all-pervading Brahman (*pronounced as Brhmn*) and how comprehending, realizing and merging with Brahman is the ultimate goal for every individual.

Comprehending Brahman

Brahman is beyond the grasp of five senses, mind and intellect, however sacred these may be, so these cannot reveal or explain 'That' Brahman. These faculties help or lead an aspirant to only some extent, as the realm of Brahman transcends all these faculties of *jiva*.

Hence, Brahman is inscrutable, incomprehensible and one which can't be readily interpreted, understood or investigated by body, mind and intellect of an individual.

This is the reason why most of the time logical and analyzing faculties of mind and intellect of the jivas aren't able to convince themselves about Brahman. Jivas generally try to figure-out Brahman through their minds and intellect, whereas Brahman is beyond all these attributes.

Though, all the sacred texts have tried to demystify the all-pervading Brahman, one can only get an idea about the same because Brahman is something to be experienced and is beyond knowledge and comprehension.

The sacred phrase *'atmaivaish iteev'* (i.e. The Self alone is all this) pronounces that the non-dual Brahman has appeared as the sum totality of animate and inanimate forms in the universe.

Though Brahman is devoid of all senses, yet it witnesses It's own creation with absolute intelligence, as without the aid of either of the senses or sense organs, It can see, hear, taste, smell and feel.

It is the truth that the proclaimation *'Brahman appears as all this'* is not easily grasped by the limited faculties of mind because Brahman is beyond the grasp of five senses, mind and intellect.

As Brahman is endowed with such unimaginable powers, It's true nature is a subject for endless discussions and attention.

However, it can be understood that Brahman is the cause of liberation of all beings and is present in all beings, rendering them conscious.

Creation does have a beginning and it all started as a vibration of the sound Om. The appearance of formless Reality as form (in the form of universes comprising of animate and inanimate forms) is only a phenomenon and it does not involve evolution or transformation, as is commonly believed.

This is so because evolution or transformation requires cause-effect relationship but Brahman is eternal and beyond the cause-effect relationship.

This whole universe which is comprehensible by body, mind, intellect and their related faculties is a manifestation of Brahman, itself. So, this universe is Brahman only but, Brahman is not only this universe but beyond all this.

Even while one is a part and parcel of the universe and its appearance, one can attain bliss by negation of the manifestation and 'realizing the background', on which this manifestation has appeared.

By negation is meant the negation of all that is comprehended by the triad of body, mind and intellect and their related faculties.

Therefore, if one negates the existence of this whole world as being illusory, it becomes easier to attain the Brahmic Bliss.

The Upanishads reveal and affirm that the Almighty Shiva is the Lord of Gods and that His Being is the sole basis of one and all. He is the One enthusiastically praised and lauded by the Vedas as the state of non-dual bliss, transcending the five sheaths i.e. food, vital air, mind, intellect and bliss.

However dominantly substantial and real the world phenomenon might appear, it is only an effect, and it can't in any way generate the cause, which is the Brahman. It is the sole cause of all the worldly phenomenon.

All the Vedas and Upanishads glorify the Lord *Mahesvara* as the ultimate Truth, the Infinite and bestower of bliss. However, those who are ignorant of this basic fact keep reveling falsely in the illusory happiness of worldly activities.

This *avidya* (lack of knowledge) results in their illusory joy, just as a thirsty person feels ecstatic joy on sensing presence of water in a mirage but such joy is false and short-lived.

Desires are a result of absence of enquiry and these very desires result in various good or bad karmas, thereby leading to the vicious cycle of rebirth and transmigration of the soul. The transmigration continues till an individual jiva gets liberated.

It is important to understand and contemplate on the below:

- ✓ Brahman is the stabilizing tail of the entire *jagat* i.e. universe. Once everything is annihilated, only the Almighty *Mahesvara* remains because He is inexhaustible. He is Brahman.

- ✓ Brahman is seated in the body (of all animate species) as Heart-space (physical heart isn't being referred to here) causing rise of elemental space, in which the world is lodged.

✓ Everything consisting the universe i.e. animate, inanimate, body, mind, intellect etc. gets resolved into the Primal Source i.e. Lord Shiva at the time of universal ending, dissolution or annihilation.

✓ All that is comprehended by body, mind and intellect and their attributes is 'unreal'. Brahman alone is 'not unreal'. Brahman alone is all that is heard, seen or felt by bodily sensory capabilities or comprehended by mind and intellect.

Brahman described

Though it is not possible to describe or comprehend the Brahman through body, mind, intellect and related faculties, yet sacred scriptures have tried to provide an idea or a hazy picture of Brahman.

Brahman can be better understood, comprehended and contemplated after knowing the nature of Brahman.

The nature of the Brahman can be described as below:

- ✓ This world is a manifestation of Brahman alone. Without world, Brahman is but without Brahman, there can be no manifestation and therefore no world.

- ✓ Brahman appears as the diverse forms because of the limiting adjuncts i.e. capabilities of senses, mind and intellect. When all this is realized only as an illusion, nothing exists by its own virtue.

- ✓ Brahman alone shines as the senses, the objects and the behaviors and activities. All joy and all knowledge personified is Brahman alone.

- ✓ The operation of worldly *Maya* (illusion) is said to be Brahman alone.

Brahman alone is the great mystic design, the whole world, the sentient and the insentient, the attributes and qualities.

Brahman is the limitless Self, the transcendental bliss, the supreme knowledge, the object, the beings and whatever little there is, is Brahman alone.

Brahman alone is the ultimate shore, the triad of states (waking, sleep and dreaming), the multiplicity, the supreme transcendence, the body, the form and the formless, senses of sound, smell, touch, the mind and the essence.

The secretive, the external, the eternal are all Brahman alone.

The beginning and end of the world and the state of the beginning and end of the world as well as the beings and non-beings are all Brahman alone.

Truth and existence, waking, dreaming, deep sleep and *turiya* (fourth state) are Brahman only. The before and the beyond, the complete and the eternal, the manifested are all Brahman only.

The joyous Brahman is manifesting everywhere as the adorable form. The individual exhibiting *Satvik* (pure and auspicious) tendencies shines as Shiva always.

- It is Brahman alone that is realized through meditation and the accomplishment of all the yogas is also said to be Brahman only.

- Brahman alone shines as the world, as the people, as the form, assembly of sages and forms of meditation.

Brahman alone is forms of Divine, as absolute and relative knowledge, pure and the enlightened Self, the *Paramesvara*.

> Brahman alone is the highest bliss, the expanding light of consciousness, the highest knowledge.

- ➢ Brahman alone is the Self of the living beings, the form of sacrifice, the sacred offering. All is indeed Brahman alone.

- ➢ Brahman alone is the whole world, the Guru and disciple, all the accomplishments, all the mantras, japa and all the actions.

- ➢ Brahman alone is all peacefulness, the core of heart, all unitariness, the state of imperishable and the attribute of imperishable.

- ➢ Whatever supreme there is, is Brahman alone, the great devotion and objective knowledge.

Without doubt, Brahman is all - this entire world, you and whatever there is. All is indeed Brahman.

- ➢ Brahman alone is only Brahman, the Self, by itself, is only Bliss and is all so attainable. Brahman alone is all, only Brahman and anything apart from Brahman is ever unreal.

- ➢ Brahman alone is the import of all sacred utterances, the supreme state, truth and untruth, devoid of beginning and end, the one eternal joy, bliss of consciousness. Brahman alone is the One, without any doubt.

- ➢ Brahman alone is Consciousness itself, self-abiding, rid of adjuncts or attributes, the eternal all, all that is pure, ever easily accomplished, the truth of truths.

➢ Brahman alone is happiness, verily happiness, the blissful Self, the ever spoken of.

➢ Brahman alone is the complete Brahman, the one witness of all, the lavish abode, the all-round perfect Self, the undiminishing essence, the devotion, the Self of all beings, the embodiment of happiness and the eternally satisfied Self.

➢ Brahman alone is the Self that is non-dual only, the ethereal space-like *Isvara*, the joy of heart. There is nothing higher than Brahman and apart from Brahman, there is no world either.

Apart from Brahman, nothing is, you are not you, and there is no joy, no fruit, not a blade of grass.

Any state apart from Brahman is a myth. The world apart from Brahman is an illusion. There is nothing apart from Brahman. All is indeed Brahman alone.

Any action, body, mind, intellect, egoity, this world apart from Brahman is a myth and an illusion. All is indeed Brahman alone.

~ *Om Namah Shivay* ~

3. Consciousness

While the last chapter dealt at the macro-level i.e. the Brahman, this chapter brings it back to the individual jiva level for more detailed comprehension of the Jnana i.e. the knowledge.

Bhagwan Shiva proclaimed it thus:

God and individual *jiva* are the result of the duality that is visible or comprehensible at the body, mind, intellect level but the same duality doesn't exist in the unitary state of Consciousness *(chaitnya)*.

Consciousness, the awareness *(chetna)*, the supreme wisdom or the supreme intelligence is none other than the Lord Shiva.

After the death of physical body of the *jiva* i.e. final dissolution of gross body and withdrawal of senses, this Consciousness leaves the body in a subtle form to rest in the Immutable.

By the graceful grace of Lord Shiva, at the time of rebirth i.e. the succeeding cycle of birth and death of gross body, the individual 'awakes' to illusorily enjoy the apparently new round of world of materials. This happens owing to this Consciousness entering the body of jiva.

So effectively, physical birth and death isn't about vital airs entering or leaving the body; but it is about Consciousness entering or leaving physical body.

Consciousness is the essence, the Light, and the power that animates the physical body.

Consciousness / Awareness

The duality of 'I' and 'you', 'this and 'that', 'one' or 'second' or 'many', good or bad, high or low, and birth or death etc. is all illusory.

This is all Consciousness alone and all is full of that Awareness indeed. All world is consciousness alone.

Earth, water, fire, air, space, ether, Brahma, Vishnu, Shiva – are all full of Awareness indeed.

'Your being', 'my being', 'everyone's being' are also Consciousness alone. There is not an iota outside it.

If there is no Awareness, then nothing is and with Awareness only, everything is. This Awareness alone renders everything knowable, comprehendable or perceivable for an individual. This Awareness is Consciousness alone.

> The past, present and the future, the matter and the time are all Consciousness only.

Knowledge, knowable and known are Awareness only. All is only Awareness indeed.

➢ Truth and untruth, beginning and end are all Consciousness alone. Talk, speech, and hearing are Consciousness only.

By its very being, a thing is full of Consciousness, ever.

➢ If there are *Brahma, Vishnu and Mahesh,* they are indeed Consciousness alone. Similarly, celestials, humans, animals, gods and demons, Guru and disciple are all Being (sat) i.e. Consciousness alone.

➢ Even the seer and the seen, the knower and the known, the fixed and the unfixed, the fabulous and the ugly are all Consciousness alone. The body is indeed only Consciousness.

➢ Even the *linga* (symbol), the cause and the effect, the form and the formlessness, the virtue and the sin are all Consciousness alone.

➢ Duality and non-duality, the Vedas and the Vedanta, the directions and the directionless and their protectors and guardians are all Consciousness only.

- ➢ Behaviours of the past, present and future are awareness alone. Name and form, beings and world are only consciousness.

- ➢ Vital air *(Prana)* is indeed Consciousness alone. All the senses, the five sheaths *(panchkosha)* and such are only Consciousness.

- ➢ Only Consciousness is bliss and the eternal and the ephemeral are Consciousness alone.

All is certainly Consciousness and there is nothing eternal or truthful but only Consciousness.

Consciousness i.e. Awareness is Brahman alone.

There is no bondage, no liberation but Consciousness alone. The only reality is Consciousness alone.

~ Om Namah Shivay ~

4. Knowledge

Having understood the why and how of beginning of the *Shristi* i.e. universe and then Brahman and Consciousness (*chetna or chaitnya*) being Lord Shiva himself, it is very important to know and understand what is worth knowing and who is truly knowable?

Lord Shiva addressed this basic question of every spiritual seeker or aspirant, thus:

What is worth knowing?

'Self alone is worth knowing' and Bliss has its origin in the Self i.e. Bhagwan Shiva.

This 'knowledge' can't be gained even in a hundred lives till:

- ✓ the mystery of triads is not comprehended,

- ✓ consciousness, the supreme wisdom, doesn't appear to be the primal cause (though in realty it is),

- ✓ and till a well-guided effort to gain this knowledge is taken-up in full earnest through spiritual path.

This implies that *'Jnana'* i.e. knowledge isn't a function of time but is dependent upon the efforts of the individual.

One individual *jiva* may go through hundreds of rebirths or transmigratory cycles and not gain even an iota of *Jnana*, while another individual *jiva* may attain *Jnana* in one lifetime itself through well-guided earnest efforts.

'Knowledge' (*Jnana*) can only be the result of a conscious, meaningful and systematically well-guided practice and one shouldn't expect it as a consequence of a specified number of lives or a defined period of time.

Conclusively, it results from 'active', well-guided endeavour and not from a 'passive', time-bound programme.

Intensity of effort in the right direction, perseverance and devotion, and an able guidance determines the speed with which the outcome (attaining the knowledge of the Self i.e. *atma-jnana*) is achieved.

'Who is Knowable'?

Lord Skanda answered it thus as a direct proclamation from Isvara:

It is the supreme Almighty Shiva, who emerges as the killer of death upon the annihilation of entire *shristi* (universe), and 'That' alone is knowable as a result of spiritual practice.

Lord Shiva is Brahman alone and therefore if one has attained *Brahman-Jnana* (knowledge of Brahman), then the goal i.e. liberation from this transmigratory cycle is attained and one abides in Brahman alone.

The Almighty operates this Grace at His will and ever remains unquestionable.

Though karma and other subtle causes can and do affect the world or an individual *jiva* but none of this can effect or influence Him, the Lord Shiva.

The Light

Air is subtle than earth and water so it pervades them. Similarly space is subtle than air, earth and water, so it pervades all three. These five elements and their related attributes are all in the universe of body, mind and intellect.

The expanded consciousness is subtle than the universe of body, mind and intellect. Therefore, consciousness pervades all these.

However, the Light that lights the universe including the consciousness is subtler than the expanded consciousness itself.

No one can count, imagine or reckon it, as it eludes numbers, computing or scientific logic of intellect. It is called 'svabhav' – the Being-ness of oneself.

This Being-ness or 'svabhav' is the one which expresses itself in each individual in a myriad ways, projects every moment and forever in countless worlds of joy.

Anything conceived by the five senses supported by the triad of body, mind, intellect or five vital airs can't be the Light, that is Consciousness.

In effect, in spite of being mediated by the resources (body, mind and intellect) of oneself, the spiritual effort involves the freedom of oneself from such media or resources of body, mind and intellect.

In the realm of knowledge relating to the Light, *sat* (the basis of existence of universe) is appreciated and experienced as 'Being-ness' i.e. I-ness, yet while expressing, it is expressed as 'You alone are, O Lord'.

Such devotion transcending the duality is required to know this Light.

~ Om Namah Shivay ~

5. Apparent Duality

Human intellect, along with the attributes and capabilities of body and mind, is limited to comprehending the world and its components only; but the origin and originator of this world and its components are beyond the scope of human intellect.

It is not possible to explain or discriminate between *Isvara* (God) and *jiva* (combination of physical and subtle body) and *jagat* (entire universe that is comprehended by all humans and their body, minds and intellect) without being rooted in the spirit of the tetrad of the great aphorisms i.e. *mahavakyas*.

Four aphorisms i.e. one from each of the Vedas and their Upanishads are called the *Mahavakyas*. These *mahavakyas* reveal the nature of Atma i.e. Self and Brahman i.e. the Divine. They are:

1. *Prajnanam Brahman* i.e. Consciousness is Brahman. It has been taken from the Rig Veda and appears in Aitarya Upanishad.

2. *Aham Brahman-Asmi* i.e. the Self is Brahman. It has been taken from the Yajur Veda and appears in Brihadaranyaka Upanishad.

3. *Tat-tvam-asi* i.e. You are That. It has been taken from the Sam Veda and appears in the Chandogaya Upanishad.

4. *Ayam-atma Brahman* i.e. The Atma is Brahman. It has been taken from the Atharva Veda and appears in the Mandukya Upanishad.

These *mahavakyas* i.e. great aphorisms are interpreted as supporting the proclamation and insight that the individual self (*jiva*) which appears as a separate existence, is an essence (*atma*) and part and manifestation of the whole i.e. Brahman, the *Param-Atma*.

The subtle body is not even remotely comparable to *Isvara*, the Light of transcendence. Those who believe that their transient body (the physical body whom they comprehend as self and truth) is the truth and imagine their life, bliss, glory and hope lies in this transient body and this world are nowhere closer to *Isvara*, the only source.

Such individuals, even if equipped with subtlest of intellect, can't comprehend the significance and value of the *mahavakyas*.

One can attain all forms of joy related to body, mind, and intellect in this world except the bliss of Brahman.

For the bliss of Brahman, one has to go beyond body, mind and intellect.

The distinction between *jiva* and *Isvara* may seem to be existing but can't be comprehended and overcome without reconciling oneself with the teachings of the Vedas and Upanishads.

Sometimes it is said and believed that the 'Self' is the real 'Doer' of all actions, yet actually in the Self, there is no action to begin with.

All actions take place in the universal presence of Lord Shiva. It is He who causes the enactment of the inanimate and animate forms of the universe and the multifarious actions and actors thereof.

The Supreme Lord plays the role of Guru (guiding light) steering the three worlds towards salvation by impregnating each and every atom of every inanimate and animate form, in each and every imaginable space in the universe.

For the ordinary humans, the duality of *jiva* (oneself) and *Isvara* (God) is too real to be overcome and even though one has originated from the Source, one refuses to acknowledge or accept it, in spite of this fact being mentioned in the sacred scriptures.

Lord Shiva taught his son Kumara on the apparent duality thus:

- ✓ This world neither manifested ever, nor exists, and nor does it exist by itself ever.

- ✓ This world, which is comprehended as a wonder, doesn't exist. This phenomenal world, the mind, the ego-sense, the individuality (i.e. the I-ness) never exists. Brahman being alone, all these are non-existent, ever.

- ✓ There is no doer, no action, no instrument i.e. body and also there is no fear or fatigue or other effects of worldly illusions. You, being Brahman alone, all these do not exist.

- ✓ Neither there is 'One' nor any 'double'. There is neither listening nor reflection nor comprehension nor one-pointedness of mind. There is no *mantra, tantra,* illusions and delusions. Unquestioningly, you are Brahman alone.

- ✓ The two types of absorption in *Samadhi* do not exist nor does the one who measures or the measurements. The Brahman being alone, none exist.

- ✓ Certainly ignorance doesn't exist, nor does story of non-discrimination. The tetrad of related adjuncts or the triad of connections do not exist. Brahman being alone, all these are naught, ever.

- ✓ Past and future do not exist. In fact, even the present is completely absent. *Ganga, Gaya* or other sacred places and the related rituals or other things do not exist. Brahman alone is.

✓ There is no earth, no water, no fire, no air and no space anywhere. Neither are the celestials nor the guardians of directions, nor father nor *Guru* anywhere. Brahman being alone, all these are naught, ever.

✓ There is no distance i.e. far or near, no end, no middle nor any position whatsoever. There is no unity, no duality, no truth or untruth here.

✓ There is neither liberation nor bondage nor any need for declaration. There are no 'somewhere', 'something', 'real or unreal', 'pleasure or pain' etc. Brahman being alone, none exist.

✓ There are no pairs of opposites, rituals, self and non-self, generation and growth, death and the illusion of coming and going i.e. birth and rebirth.

✓ There is no 'here', no 'hereafter', no guru, no disciple. Real and unreal, existence and non-existence, duty and completed action are all non-existent.

✓ Race, caste, convention, self-discipline, physical and mental restraints do not exist. Brahman alone is.

✓ 'All is illusion', 'Brahman alone is', 'Consciousness alone is', 'I am Consciousness' - all these thoughts, words and aphorisms certainly don't exist. Brahman being alone nothing ever exists, not even the declarations – 'I am', 'I am eternal' etc.

✓ Whatever is conveyed through speech, contemplated and understood by mind, determined by intellect, unified through Yoga, performed through senses, the states of waking, dream, sleep or the fourth transcendental state are all non-existent. This is to be realized.

✓ There is never any purification through holy waters nor any sanctity through meditation.

The triad of qualities (*gunas*) doesn't exist in the least nor do the combination of the triad of qualities (personality or individuality).

The comprehension of 'one', 'two' or 'many' is an illusion.

Worldly or any illusion or the lack of it are indeed non-existent. Know it certain that nothing in the least exists and these being Brahman alone, nothing in the least remains.

How to overcome this apparent duality?

To begin with, one can develop a sympathetic attitude towards the sacred scriptures and this humble beginning will help in removing this duality in the long run.

For all the universes, the pure and unmanifest Self is the background. Only on this background all the manifestation happen and comprehended.

It is easy to understand this with the example of a movie running on a white screen. The screen is the permanent aspect whereas the movie, its actors, story, those watching movie are all manifestations and transient. Similarly, in a gold-bracelet, gold is the permanent aspect whereas bracelet is just a manifestation and transient aspect.

To a human, trivial and transitory worldly happiness seems as if it is the joy of Brahman. Even for such unillumined one; Shiva, the Self, is the cause because - He is the actual cause of whatever is perceived or experienced by both the illumined as well as unillumined.

The Sun rises and sets for those who perceive it as such but in reality the Sun never rises or sets but remains as it is i.e. shining bright always.

Dependence on bodily senses, mind and intellect results in comprehension of God separate from one-'Self'. But these tools of comprehension i.e. body, mind and intellect are themselves forms of the

Almighty Lord Shiva, which have resulted from manifestation of 'His will' alone. So, how can there be anything separate from 'Self'?

Therefore, this apparent duality is unreal, untrue and not eternal, as it is a result of ignorance. This duality vanishes as soon as one is bestowed with *atma-jnana* i.e. knowledge of the Self.

Mahesvara is the ultimate illuminator of the universe and this has been stated several times in various sacred texts and there are lot of *chhandas* i.e. passages describing the glories of the inimitable, transcended, unparalleled and exalted Lord Shiva.

Denying, giving-up and abandoning the unreal

Once an individual starts comprehending the unreality of this world and its Maya, one needs to start giving-up the unreal. Giving-up or abandoning the unreal will result in leaving behind only what is real.

After giving-up the unreal, always abiding in the real i.e. Brahman is advised in the Vedas and other sacred scriptures.

Therefore, one should always comprehend and reflect on the below:

- ✓ Everything is illusory, as everything is based on thought, which itself is non-existent. All is only consciousness indeed.

- ✓ The existence of thought-force, of mind, of Brahman or any different state; of body, of signs, of any decaying states of body; the seen, the seeing, the seer; the doer, the inspirer of action, and the deed – are all illusory.

- ✓ Oneness, duality, separateness, concepts such existence and nonexistence; variance in texts, in Vedas, the different concepts of liberation; the distinctions of species, of castes, of purity and impurity – are all illusory.

- ✓ The mode of undivided form, the supreme and undivided essence, contradictory thoughts of high and low, virtue and sin, imaginary and non-imaginary – are all illusory.

- ✓ The attained, the attainable and the means thereof, destruction, the disposition as Brahman – are all illusory.

- ✓ Knowledge relating to internal senses, the subjugation of the external senses, all appointed times of instruction, identity, residue, the lofty emanation, earth, water, fire, air, space, mind and intellect – are all unreal and illusory.

- ✓ Cause and diversity of effects, interpretations of the spiritual methods, 'All is Brahman', none of these are of the nature of reality, not even in the least.

✓ There is never anything in the name of truth. Doubt, contradiction and the cause of will are all only misapprehensions.

Since the mind and intellect are illusory, anything and everything that arises from these are also illusory.

There is nothing in this world whatsoever as anything and everything is illusory, being based on non-existent thoughts.

Real and unreal, truth and untruth, cause and effect, doer, enjoyer and action are all non-existent, without doubt. There is nothing to be enjoyed nor there any contentment of enjoyment.

Therefore, renounce 'I am the body' thought and be of the conviction that 'I am Brahman alone' and be ever of the certitude and always be established thus:

o I am not the individual, have no differences, have neither thought nor mind, have neither flesh nor bones nor body with ego.

o I am neither the one who measures nor that is measured. I am not all. I am the supreme, of the form of complete knowledge.

- o I am neither the dead nor another life, nor just consciousness, nor that which is spoken of, nor the liberated, nor the enlightened, ever.

- o I am neither emptiness nor am I a fool. I am transcendent. I am Brahman alone, ever.

- o Therefore, forsaking everything, remain like a wall. Be of the certitude that 'I am Brahman alone' and be of the disposition – 'I alone am'.

- o Always be of the certitude that I alone am, nothing else. I am Bliss, Consciousness, and Brahman alone.

- o I am taintless, pure, and different from the individual soul, the Self of all, shining as 'I', Brahman alone. I alone am, just consciousness, the attributeless, the ever auspicious.

Denying the apparent duality between individual *jiva* and *Isvara* by comprehending the illusory nature of this world and its attributes; and then abiding in the certitude – 'I am Brahman alone' leads to liberation from the transmigratory cycle of rebirth.

~ Om Namah Shivay ~

6. The Self

Lord Shiva is the Self, while universe is the other i.e. non-Self. The whole manifestation is a projection of the Self and there can be no distinction between the two. So, the apparent duality is non-existent.

The life-current traverses the body in a cyclic fashion i.e. with a distinct beginning and end, which is referred to as birth and death. However, the Self is eternal.

Though the gross or extroverted mind cannot comprehend the Self, the Self reveals itself to the discriminative and disciplined mind. Shiva is that Self of all.

Experience of the Self is similar for all those who have been able to experience it. However, the qualification and approach of the seeker can cause variability in its expression.

If ordinary sense enjoyments can defy description or result in varying degrees of variations in descriptions, how can there be any uniformity in describing the experience of the Self, which is the mother of all the experiences.

The final goal i.e. abiding in the Self or Self-Realisation is the absolutely thought-free state, so any conceptualisation of this state will be self-contradictory.

No science or logic or numbers or analysis can ever reveal the eternal Self. Being within, it needs to be found by a meticulous pursuit involving one's mind and intellect.

A mind that is introverted by self-enquiry and a thorough investigation into the mind, which has been already ripened by unsullied and relentless self-discipline.

The Self as the reason for divergent faiths

In the gross world, the five sense organs of a jiva and the attributes of mind are the driving forces of the body.

The mind is the interface between the gross world and the transcendental self.

In the course of discharging its power to the mind, the Self assumes an affinity to the vital airs (Prana) and other elements, which are precursors of the senses.

Though the Self is eternal, pure and enlightened, yet this phenomenon of the Self being entangled in the inert world led to a plethora of divergent faiths and contradictory philosophies.

Each faith or philosophy has been trying to account for or describe this phenomenon as per their own capabilities, comprehension and intellect leading to contradictions or the divergences.

Nature of the Self

The self is devoid of attributes, adjuncts etc. and transcends space-time frame of reference and limitations. It is as it is.

To limit it by describing its form or nature is an illusion itself. Like space, it penetrates the innermost recesses of everything, including space itself, and yet, it ever remains unmodified.

The Self is not different in diverse bodies of jivas. By its very nature, it is spread-out throughout everything.

Just as the same electricity runs the fan, lights the bulb and powers an engine, the Self mobilises the inert world, including bodies.

Though the actors in the world are the inert or gross bodies, all actions are ascribed to the Self. In spite of this, the Self is not the enjoyer in the ordinary sense.

When *jiva* acquires body by past karma, the embodied or the manifested Self is dubbed as the experiencer of the pains and pleasures.

It lasts until the demise of the gross body. The body being gross, gets destroyed while the Self, being eternal, is released.

An individual's identification with his / her body, mind and intellect is *ajnana* (ignorance) whereas a seeker's comprehending and realizing one's true 'Self' is the true *jnana* (knowledge).

The Self can be further explained thus:

- ✓ The Self is of the form of dual and nondual, bereft of duality and nonduality, void of everything.

- ✓ The Self is of the nature of happiness and unhappiness, liberated, divine, and thought-free essence. There is not a whit besides the Self.

- ✓ The Self is unblemished, immaculate, intelligent, primordial, blissful, birthless, incalculable, measurable, and immortal and the past, present and future.

- ✓ Besides the Self, there is nothing that exists.

- ✓ The Self is conceivable, inferred by imagination, transcendental and serene, ever directly present, ever directly proven, of the nature devoid of otherness. And is all that is. There is nothing besides the Self.

- ✓ The Self is ever directly visible, ever directly proven and of the nature devoid of otherness, devoid of unreality with nothing besides It. It is certainly Itself *Isvara*.

- ✓ The pure 'Self' is neither knowledge nor ignorance, neither has any dimension nor is dimensionless, is devoid of permanence and impermanence.

- ✓ The Self is devoid of the gross body and is without subtle body as well as without a casual body.

- ✓ The Self is devoid of being comprehended as the seen, is without beginning, middle or end. The peaceful Self is void of *Samadhi*. There is nothing besides the Self.

- ✓ The Self is perfect and of the form of Bliss, ever devoid of waking or dream state.

- ✓ The Self is the past and the future, is imperishable and of the form of consciousness, without beginning, middle or end.

- ✓ The Self is without all types of resolutions (*sankalp*), ever pure, just awareness and undiminishing, devoid of knower, knowable and such.

- ✓ The singular Self, the Self devoid of one, is ever bereft of duality and nonduality. The Self is natural and oneself.

- ✓ The *turiya* (fourth state) Self is also the eternal Self and whatever little is here, it is the Self. The Self is the honourable and without honour.

- ✓ The Self is all and without all, rejoicing within, it is the joy of speech.

Total abidance in the Self is possible after eradication of ignorance (*ajnana*). Fluctuations of mind caused by unchecked senses is the hindrance in realising the Self.

These fluctuations of mind lead to fatigue of mind making it incapable to enter the Heart-space, the seat of the Self. Heart-space shouldn't be confused with the physical heart.

These hindrances can be overcome by constantly cleaning the mind of this unwanted traffic.

All that is mind-born is verily the Self. All this world, all this happiness is only the Self.

Everything, including the Self is Brahman, only consciousness. Bliss is the highest measure and all this world, which is visible, is nothing at all.

Self is all that is worth knowing because all the illusion of the body, mind and intellect and this world vanishes as soon as one gains the knowledge of the Self i.e. *atma-vidya*.

'Knowledge of the Self' is what is generally referred to as the Self-Realization or *Moksha* or liberation from the transmigratory cycle of rebirths.

Therefore, one should endeavour to acquire the Knowledge of the Self through study of sacred texts, *atma-vichar* (self-enquiry), *Vivek* (discriminating between real and unreal) and constantly asking oneself – 'Who am I'?

~ Om Namah Shivay ~

7. Glories of Mahadeva

All the sacred texts have glorified, eulogised and praised the Almighty Shiva, the *Paramatma*. Glories of the Mahadeva in the sacred texts are explained in this chapter.

Mahesvara Himself represents himself in various forms and therefore listening to his glories or meditating on either or all of those forms results in abidance in the Lord Himself.

The Vedas and Upanishads endorse such practices and establish the inseparable union of universe and its Lord Shiva and the supremacy of the *Vishvanath (Lord of the world)*.

Fundamental principle behind all the activities of *jiva* is *Prana* i.e. life-force and since Parmesvara is the bestower of Prana, the supremacy or lordship of Him is proved beyond doubt.

There is no animate or inanimate object which is not endowed and blessed by the omnipotent, omnipresent, omniscient and absolute *Isvara*.

Shiva is the Self while the entire universe is the other-Self, with the whole universe being a manifestation of the will of the Self i.e. a projection of the Self itself.

Therefore, there can be no distinction between the two. Whatever distinction is comprehended is because of ignorance *(avidya).*

The life-force traverses the body with a distinct beginning and end in a cyclic fashion and operates in a similar way in the outer world also.

This Self and its unlimited expanse is incomprehensible by the unknowledgeable mind or intellect and extroverted senses but the Self reveals itself to the discriminative and disciplined mind, who looks within oneself. Lord Shiva is that Self of all.

The sacred texts are replete with assertions and recitations of oneness of unitary and non-dual state of existence of the Lord.

However, this makes it difficult for one to understand this unitariness because of the apparent differentiations in the universe, resulting from the triad of *gunas (sat, rajas, tamas)* or varying subtleties or grossness of matter.

Individual *jiva* comprehends these differentiations owing to the multitude combinations of gunas which manifest as differing personalities to the ignorant *jiva.*

Due to his ignorance, *jiva* doesn't comprehend and realise that these gunas, subtleties or grossness of matter and resulting differences are all manifestations of the Supreme Lord.

Cause of creation may be falsely taken as intercourse between the feminine and masculine forms. But intercourse is only the tool for procreation and multiplication of races.

The real causative force in the field of creation is the *Sakti* (power) of Lord Shiva, which is present everywhere, including in the field of creation and the feminine and masculine forms.

> Lord Shiva is the consciousness of all beings and sole enjoyer of all the fruits. Though the world is mortal, Lord Shiva is eternal i.e. beginingless and endless.

> *Paramesvara* Shiva is the indweller as well as vanquisher of death and the inspirer of souls towards action. He relentlessly proves and establishes himself in every form and state of existence.

> According to Vedas, *Mahesvara* is the sole destroyer of the vicious cycle of rebirth and transmigration. At the same time, Upanishads explain that it is Lord Shiva who is the cause of various states of existence in diverse forms of being both an 'enjoyer' and 'enjoyment'.

> Bhagwan *Shankara* is vigorously, ostentatiously and gracefully growing everywhere into the animate, the inanimate, the infinite (*Isvara*) and the fierceful

(*Rudra*). In the finite animate forms, He is the consciousness.

> *Shambhu* means the embodiment of joy, the giver of happiness. Upanishads state this fact as '*Kam Brahman Kham Brahman*' (*ka* meaning happiness and *kha* meaning space) i.e. Happiness is Brahman and Space is Brahman.

> The wise (those bestowed with knowledge) contemplate on these words and their imports, thereby assimilating the truth of Shiva.

> Shiva, the heart-throb of *Maa Uma*, is the indweller of all and all reside in His expansiveness and therefore nothing is beyond the *Vishvanath*.

> However, the *avidya* i.e. ignorance of the *jiva* is proved by the fact this that they are blind to Him, who is the most intimate one in themselves, within their hearts.

However, a systematic or logical study of the sacred texts can never settle all the doubts of *jiva*.

The wise one (*jnani*) never resorts to one's own intelligence but always seeks Bhagwan Shiva's grace to understand and comprehend the Vedic texts and their imports.

Without *Paramatma's* Grace, it is not possible to comprehend the import of the Vedas and all other sacred texts because their import is beyond the capability of the body, mind and intellect of any *jiva*.

The Almighty operates this Grace at His will and ever remains unquestionable.

Though karma and other subtle causes can and do affect the world or an individual *jiva* but none of this can effect or influence Him, the Lord Shiva.

Experience of the Lord Shiva

Almighty Shiva is what is described in the *Sastras* i.e. sacred texts as well as beyond them.

If and when conflicting descriptions appear in the sacred texts, the same needs to be understood in proper context and not discarded or create a controversy out of the same.

The truth of Lord Shiva (who is truth himself), the Brahman or Consciousness given in various sacred texts is of transcendental nature and beyond comprehension of faculties of body, mind or intellect.

All the descriptions, including those given by the enlightened ones, are only symbolic in nature and needs to be treated as sign-posts on the route to comprehend the ultimate Bhagwan Shiva.

A wise man of *Vivek* (discriminative ability) derives guidance from the sacred texts and strives to transcend his own mind and intellect, transcend himself and transcend the designer of all ideas of difference, thereby strive to experience Shiva, the true Self.

A lot of times, individual *jiva* wants to be logical and analytical by denying presence of the Almighty within himself or within inanimate idols, which are worshipped by millions since millions of years.

Oneness of individual jiva and the Almighty has been already established. Now, as far as, the idols are considered, these are the symbols of the Almighty, such as Lord Shiva is often symbolised as Shiv-linga and worshipped.

Though, everything and anything in this world is non-existent owing to it's illusory nature, still if an individual *jiva* wishes to seek unitariness of oneself with the Supreme through symbols, it is perfectly alright.

However, ultimately one has to transcend the body, mind, intellect faculties and abide in the supreme Brahman. When one transcends body, mind and intellect, the symbolism automatically goes away.

Till that happens, everyone is free to use free-will bestowed by the Almighty Himself to choose one's way forward in the spiritual journey, depending on the *samskara* and temperament of individual *jiva*.

The omniscient Lord Shiva and His knowledge are one. This knowledge has been explained and expanded by various sages in the spirit of various systems and as per their natural inclinations as well as impact of the cosmic cycles during which these sages took birth.

Such divergent explanations and interpretations have given rise of various systems of philosophy but the central theme i.e. the final aim of all these remain the same i.e. union with the Brahman or *Isvara*.

It is any seeker's great fortune that he acquires deep desire and devotion for union with 'Shiva, the Almighty' and contemplates and meditates with Him as the sole *lakshay* i.e. aim.

One who does so is certain to be bestowed His protection and transcend the rebirth (birth-death cycles) through removal of *avidya* i.e. ignorance.

Being of the certitude 'I am Brahman' and always abiding in the certitude 'I am Brahman' will ultimately result in being established in Brahman.

Love and Devotion emphasised

Those who recite the Vedas or practice hath yoga or practice spirituality 'without' the loving devotion to the lotus feet of the blue-throated Lord are not only not liberated but get tormented and their agonies intensified even after death. They return to this world of dire pain and keep roaming around begging for food.

The pure love and devotion for the Lord Shambhu never generates in a life in fleeting momentary worldly pleasures. Such ignorant people fall to increasingly pathetic realms and experience a long vicious rebirth cycle.

Such *jivas* are so ignorant that they don't devote their hearts to the devotion of the Lord but keep experiencing hell of worldly pains.

Sometimes, by chance, they may be born among the illiterate idiots and pose likewise, get to dabble in scriptures, learn to please the demigods by means of *mantras*, *bijaksharas* or sacrificial offerings.

But such ignorant jivas refuse to serve with pure hearts the conferrer of liberation Lord *Shambhu*. Such ignorant ones are never liberated.

On the other hand, there are those seekers whose minds gradually turn away from worldly objects and pleasures and draw nearer to the Self, who take delight in worship of Shivalinga and establish the Almighty Shiva in their hearts, propitiating him in good as well as bad times.

Such seekers have their mind established in their ideal, Lord Shiva and they overcome worldly and spiritual hurdles easily by His grace.

Such seekers wear the *tripunt* (triple strips) of *bhasma* on their forehead and also smear it on their body, along with wearing *rudraksh* garlands and armbands.

They keep remembering Shambhu by chanting His name, *mantras or bijaksharas* and pass their time in the services of the Almighty, worshipping the *Shivalinga* with liberation being their final goal.

Such seekers gain union with Lord Shiva through their pure heart, devotion and reverential actions, thereby avoiding all pains of worldly life and liberation from the rebirth cycles.

Even if one learns Vedic grammar (*vyakaran*), has all the scriptural knowledge or lives in the illusory glory of mastering logic (*tarka*), rituals (*Mimamsa*), yogic postures, Vedantic texts or takes holy baths in the *Ganga or Triveni*, one doesn't gain anything without true love and devotion for Me, the *Shambhu*.

A seeker can cleanse oneself by wearing sacred ashes and worshipping, propitiating and single-mindedly devoting to Lord Shiva seeking liberation on eighth day of lunar calendar (*Ashtami*) and on mid-night of full-moon day (*Pradosh*).

Knowledge (*Jnana*) doesn't arise in those who never serve sacred Shiva centres and Shivalinga by performing holy sacrificial worship, ablutions, abhisheka along with recitation of *Sri Rudra Mantras, panchakshari mantra* etc.

Those who recite the glories and sin-effacing mantras of Lord Shiva and devotes their heart completely to Him, to such seekers this teaching (knowledge) is imparted.

Those who love their Guru and are earnestly faithful to the *Mahadeva*, the understanding and comprehension of this sacred knowledge is revealed.

This *Jnana* (knowledge) that is entrusted to such sincere seekers is nowhere to be found. Therefore, it must be protected from fools (those running after worldly objects and pleasures).

However, it can be offered to the deserving ones of purity, devotion, single-mindedness and discernment.

~ *Om Namah Shivay* ~

8. Sacred texts

Lord Shiva's exhalation resulted in the sacred Vedas and the same were received by the inhalation of the creator Lord Brahma.

Having originated from the Almighty Himself, there can be no space / occasion for argument, controversy or dispute in the authority of the Vedas. Unflinching faith and conviction in the authority of the Vedas is mandatory.

The Vedas are the oldest scriptures and therefore are the basis of all other sacred scriptures. Since they are the basis, there must be harmony among them.

If one finds some dissonances, these may be due to differences in time, place or influence of societal values during the times when these later texts were written.

It is advisable and desirable to develop a conviction in the supremacy of Almighty Shiva through sacred texts. Sacred texts, under proper guidance helps an aspirant on the spiritual journey.

Though the Vedas are described as a quartet, they are innumerable. Taking various names and forms, they have established in various geographies granting variety of fruits.

The immediate purpose of these sacred texts might appear as pertaining to the mundane, having their roots in ground, they motivate and coax the seeker into ultimate good.

Careful examination and deeper understanding of these sacred texts reveal that the true nature and purpose of these sacred works is in fact the Ultimate.

This is not clearly apparent to everyone is not because this true nature and purpose is hidden but because it is understood and comprehended differently under diverse circumstances.

Therefore, it is wise to follow the sacred texts in proper context and under able guidance, if possible.

The world is a conglomerate of *jivas* of divergent make-up living in divergent geographies under varied circumstances. The Almighty and his utterances i.e. the Vedas and sacred texts direct each jiva towards the common goal i.e. 'Self-Realisation'.

Those who reverentially follow the sacred texts with devotion, Shraddha and without doubting the ultimate aim, receive Almighty's grace.

Those discharged with the authority to take-up the study of sacred texts must do so with full adoration, trust and without expecting any materialistic fruits thereof, under teachers of purity and eminence.

Those who have gained mastery over the sacred texts, should strive to propagate their study to others and help maintain the welfare of the world.

Is studying Vedas mandatory?

To attain self-realization, studying or reciting the Vedas is not at all mandatory, though studying and comprehending the sacred texts helps one in the spiritual journey, yet it is of utmost importance to practice the sacred utterances and surrendering the outcome of the spiritual practices to Isvara.

Even without learning of the sacred texts, one can achieve liberation by direct realization of the Light of the 'Self'. By such *Vidya or Jnana* (knowledge), both spiritual and mundane worldly aspirations are achieved.

Though the experience of the Self is similar for all seekers, qualification and approach of the seeker can cause variability in expression.

Same sensory experience is generally described in differing manner by people. If sensory experience description can have such variability, then experience of the Self (the highest of all experiences), which is beyond body, mind and intellect, can never be described in similar way.

Though studying of the Vedas is not mandatory, yet the anomalies of experiences can always be settled through proclamations of the Vedas.

Is learning sacred texts enough?

However, it is not sufficient to be satisfied with learning of sacred texts only because mere learning or knowledge of texts doesn't reveal Him, the *Paramatma* because:

- ✓ Those sages who transcended the triad of body, mind and intellect proclaimed that the experience of Almighty Shiva is unique and beyond expression in written or spoken words, as these are products of the gross body only.

- ✓ Sacred texts, being the products of written and spoken words, cannot reveal true nature of the experience of the Supreme.

- ✓ Even the scriptural revelations can only provide a hazy glimpse or a distant echo of the all-transcending divine *Shivam*.

- ✓ *Paramesvara* is the bestower of transcendence i.e. release from worldly cycle for His devotees. As long as vital airs are firmly established in the gross body, there is no liberation.

✓ However, at the time of the dissolution of the body i.e. when vital airs start retreating from the gross body, the meditator (devotee) and his goal (*Isvara*) dissolve into one and this fruit thereof is said to be enjoyed by the *Paramesvara*.

✓ The devotees who could achieve union with the Self while alive are chosen by Bhagwan Shiva Himself. Such pure souls enjoy grace of Lord Shiva and remain established in one's own Self, remaining every moment aware that everything is Shiva and none else.

The universe i.e. the eternal space full of objects is a manifestation of the supreme transcendental space, just as curd is a variant of milk or vapours in clouds are variant of ocean waters. Similarly Shiva and jiva i.e. It's multitude manifestations are not-different.

➢ Even though the supreme *Paramesvara* voluntarily descends into the insignificant, infinitesimal and mortal gross body of *jiva*, He is hailed as supremely divine by the sacred texts.

➢ The omnipresent Lord Shiva, when establishes Himself in the body, is called *Purusha*. Though spread all over the gross body, His presence is found as very minute in the heart-centre by the seeker. (It is to be noted that here physical heart isn't indicated while saying heart-centre).

➢ This has been corroborated by the sacred scriptures as well as illumined sages after experiencing the same.

➢ Due to his identification with gross body, mind and intellect, worldly attractions entice and bind the *jiva*.

➢ However, once an individual is on the path of spiritual practice; *Paramatma*, the Light lighting the entire world, becomes the dominant force and inspiration for that ignorant *jiva* also.

After experiencing spiritual bliss, a seeker realises the absence of the supreme light in objective and illusory world around him, as it lacks any affinity to the Lord Shiva and his glories of knowledge, joy, blissfulness and peace.

He also realises that It's presence is within, though It transcends the body.

By entering this Light of transcendence, with utmost humility and conscious awareness, one experiences the supreme bliss of quietude, dispassion, peace and perfection.

With respect to the above primary principle, all the sacred texts are unanimous, though they may have variations regarding secondary aspects such as cosmic creation etc.

If one truly appreciates the primary principle, then one gains knowledge of the 'Self', which is pure, immortal, devoid of any gross body and is blissful.

Lord Shiva is the causeless cause of all actions and He, the Self, establishes Himself in everything i.e. the animate and the inanimate and wields the supreme power and control over the whole universe.

- ✓ All the sacred scriptures i.e. *Sruti, Smriti, Purana, Itihas, Veda and Upanishads* proclaim that *Paramesvara* is the One to be always remembered, meditated upon, loved, longed for, devoted oneself to, prayed and realised. He is unattached and beyond compare.

- ✓ Even if one wants His knowledge through direct realization, He is the one who has the supreme authority to do so and even if one wants to deny His existence, He is.

- ✓ He can't be reached by mind or intellect, but only those who are matured in spiritual practice can reach Him, by His grace alone.

Inconsistencies in sacred texts explained

The Vedas and other Sastra are flawless, unblemished and impeccable and any apparent contradictions or discrepancies are a result of faulty interpretations by immature intellects.

These sacred texts should never be disrespected and belittled.

Any apparent disagreement between the content of scriptures and experience can result from incorrect interpretation and practice and one must endeavour to clear the inconsistencies from illumined souls.

Some inconsistencies may seem too obvious to be ignored such as those relating to theories of creation, social life patterns, diverse sacred practices etc.

Other inconsistencies may have been caused due to each cosmic cycle being unique, and each having been created with some precursor elements, which will naturally differ from one to another.

One must be aware that all incongruities are in the field of phenomenon and practices only and that there are no inconsistencies as far as final aim is concerned.

There is no world without Almighty's power and will, as everything is a manifestation of His will. So, whether it appears to be flawless and blissful or full of pain and sorrow, it is His will.

Paramatma is the embodiment of perfection and still everyone has been given free-will to make oneself perfect, in whatever way or whichever time-period one wishes.

A seeker needs to make the sacred knowledge one's bow, vital airs the arrow and lose oneself by aiming for the final goal i.e. the 'Self', the blissful, flawless and pure one.

Contradictions or anomalies of phenomenon in the sacred texts have a meaning and one needs to settle them by correctly learning the sacred scriptures.

Upon gaining clarity of these anomalies, one realises that the problem lies in the perceiver and not the sacred texts.

It is quite usual for some to disregard the scriptures and scriptural knowledge based on the apparent contradictions, while more sincere seekers may either try to find reasons of the inconsistencies or disregard the inconsistencies and move ahead towards the final aim with only consistencies.

It is similar to one individual cribbing about the obstacles that he is facing in his progress, while another individual using the same obstacles as stepping stones for his successful journey.

This free-will to choose one's path as well as getting obstructed by obstacles or not has been bestowed with the individual jiva by the Almighty Shiva.

Therefore, choose it wisely and if a spiritual seeker is full of devotion, trust, faith and Shraddha, the Almighty's grace is within easy reach.

~ Om Namah Shivay ~

9. The Seeker

The one who had the desire to know the truth, the reality, the omniscient Almighty Shiva and has started working on the same is referred to as the seeker or aspirant.

The Vedas and other sacred texts have elaborated in detail on the seeker, his temperament, duties etc. This chapter has focused on the Almighty's guidance to every seeker to give clarity to some of the ever-present doubts and contradictions present in seeker's mind.

Duties of a Seeker / aspirant

Three primary duties of a seeker include:

- ✓ attaining knowledge laid down in Vedas and other sacred texts,

- ✓ overcoming or removing the shortcomings in one's svabhav and dharma with utmost patience and perseverance and lastly,

- ✓ being absolutely tolerant towards other faiths, beliefs and religions.

In addition, a seeker must completely shun the attitude of finding fault with other people or other faiths. Just as a small amount of salt can spoil an entire pot of milk, so any lenience in this duty causes a seeker's spiritual accomplishments to suffer.

If one indulges in such behaviour, he loses discrimination and consequent judgement in matters of action, inaction and non-action.

Sensory Pleasures

Vedic commandments disapprove sensory pleasures in the worldly experiences, yet some texts make promises of higher states of enjoyments to the spiritual seekers.

Such concessions are unreal and temporary but might give solace to those seekers or aspirants who lack patience and perseverance required on the spiritual path.

For those spiritual seekers who have patience and perseverance on the spiritual path, the Truth in all its simplicity and purity is revealed at appropriate time, which is neither in the enjoyment nor in the enjoyer.

One who succumbs to worldly enticements, desires and resulting fleeting pleasures land-up in a series of transmigratory lives.

Sometimes one may find mutually conflicting mandates in the sacred texts and this might create dilemma and confusion.

However, by firm conviction in the ideal One and Only Paramesvara, a seeker will gradually overcome the dilemma and spiritual progress gets restored with the mind getting reinstated into *yoga* (union of oneself with the supreme Lord).

Worldly Challenges

A spiritual seeker is not affected by the worldly life challenges, as he is convinced that he is unattached.

In due course of his spiritual practice, he realises and gets convinced that the movement of his senses into worldly objects is their nature and that he has nothing to do with the same.

It is to be remembered that one's happiness and liberation from rebirth cycles lies in following one's own unique spiritual path.

This path largely depends upon the uniqueness of one's *svabhav* (which results from a combination of 3 gunas) and *dharma* (quality which establishes one's existence), even if these appear inferior in the gross world sense.

One should never leave one's spiritual path in favour of another path. For example, a *sanyasi* might be living in forests to follow his spiritual path but if you have a family, you must fulfil your duties towards the same and use that situation itself to walk on the spiritual path.

If one leaves one's duties on the spiritual path, then one is creating karma and the same will need to be exhausted in this or subsequent births before realising the Supreme.

Righteous Actions

During one's lifetime, a seeker must discriminate between the good and the bad and by undertaking good acts, he must try to achieve the optimum output.

Celestials could achieve control over elements and achieve siddhis by overcoming the discrepancies among the sacred texts and by pushing ahead with positive inspiration.

One can do the same through one's will, *Shraddha* and devotion.

The wise sages advise that the crux of ignorance is to see the body and its actions as unrelated.

Righteous actions in the form of calm and cool perseverance in matters of social order and justice must be observed by the seeker as contrary actions bring infamy and resulting mental trauma, which hinders progress.

All sacred texts have presented these facts including the basic one that motive or intent behind one's actions results in one's honour or infamy.

Therefore, it is of paramount importance that one must be conscious of one's intent behind every action.

Strict adherence, with true faith and loyalty, to these sacred commandments outlining duties must be observed by a seeker in a disciplined way, thereby being a role model for the society.

Sacred Parables and Stories

In order to further explain certain cryptic aphorisms of the Vedas, sacred texts resort to use of examples, parables or stories.

Such parables need to be understood in proper context of Vedas, as these can be easily misunderstood in the absence of proper context. Such misunderstandings can lead to dire consequences for the seeker as well as society.

For such eventualities, true knowledge needs to be sought from the Vedas under proper guidance.

In modern times we come across a lot of examples of such misunderstandings and lot of fake, ignorant and cunning individuals pretend to be knowledgeable and misguide the gullible, ignorant masses for materialistic gains or worldly pleasures.

Also, apart from the modifications owing to improper understanding of the sacred texts, there have been additions in the sacred texts which have distorted the import or meaning of the sacred texts. A seeker needs to be careful of the same while referring to the sacred texts.

Karma Principle

Karma principle i.e. cause and effect principle is a well-tested, standardised and explained principle for the worldly life cycle. It has been variously described by various interpreters of the sacred texts.

Broadly, this principle states that all actions and intentions behind actions of an individual jiva have consequences, which will result in future situations or events of that jiva in this or future births.

Every *Karma* results in formation of *samskara* and the same needs to exhausted before one is able to find release from transmigratory cycle of rebirths, which is generally referred to as Moksha i.e. liberation.

Karma principle guides a *jiva* on how to live one's life so that he can truly become the best version of Almighty's creation that he is.

A seeker needs to adjust himself accordingly by learning to carve out a balance between this *karma* principle and the subtle and inexpressible principle i.e. the Paramesvara. Any incongruities thereof shall be settled by Lord Shiva Himself.

Worldly objects acquire differing degrees of significance based on their placement in the scheme of things of worldly affairs, which means their value is neither intrinsic nor fixed.

A seeker needs to be always consciously aware of this fact to overcome human habit of attachment or hatred. If one is able to achieve this, it greatly helps on the spiritual path.

One who doesn't rely on the fruits of destiny but continues on the spiritual path amidst the worldly tides is always blessed by the *Mahesvara* and such spiritual endeavour is upheld by the Vedas too.

A seeker must always remain unaffected by the debate as to whether the ultimate fruit is the result of one's efforts or divine blessings / grant and he must continue to strive his spiritual journey.

Instead of focusing on the results, a seeker must always remain focused on one's efforts and leave the bestowing of results to the Almighty.

From a seeker's standpoint, it needs to be remembered that there is none other than Mahadeva Shiva to grant fruits of the spiritual pursuit.

Choosing the Guru

It is advised in the sacred texts that the same needs to be learned under proper guidance and a disciple must follow his teacher always.

However, a seeker needs to be conscious of the fact that the Vedas and other sacred texts were compiled in times and context which were different from those of today.

Therefore, it is pertinent on part of the disciple to choose not only a learned and eminent but also righteous teacher.

A true teacher is able to understand and teach the sacred texts as per the aim and purpose of the sacred texts i.e. aiming for the final goal i.e. realising the Self and merging with the Almighty.

If a teacher himself is still stuck in the materialistic worldly pleasures, then he is not a teacher at all.

A seeker needs to be conscious of the fact that:

Various branches of Vedas advocate various results from various spiritual practices. Such values are assigned to the spiritual practices by Lord Shiva Himself, who is the true experience as well as the true experiencer and the supreme authority.

Isvara is the final dispenser of results of worldly actions as well as spiritual endeavour, thus is proclaimed by the Vedas.

The Vedas further explain the state of supreme bliss as well as means of attaining the same.

Lord Shiva enables comprehension and realization of these sacred theories to the one who sincerely and with a pure heart practices them.

Therefore, a seeker must always pursue his goal with pure devotion, trust, faith, and *Shraddha*.

~ Om Namah Shivay ~

10. Self-realization

In a spiritual practice, an absolutely thought-free state is the goal but even thinking about that goal involves thoughts and is therefore self-contradictory.

If knowledge of the Self is the final knowledge, then realising the Self or Self-Realization is the final aim of spiritual journey.

Lord Shiva proclaimed thus:

- ✓ Even if one is an adept Vedic proponent and practitioner, one can't get any concessions, whatsoever.

- ✓ Such a practitioner also has to develop an attitude of complete detachment from 'doer-ship' and give-up any desire for fruits of his Vedic or spiritual practices.

- ✓ Getting oneself free from the dualistic vision or illusion is the key.

- ✓ If one is regularly involved in Vedic rituals and sacrifices, one can attain heavenly realms but even in heavenly realms, distinctions similar to worldly realm are prevalent and therefore, there is pain and also end of one's time in that realm.

✓ Lot of spiritual practitioners are misguided by the lure of heaven as the result of spiritual seeking, but the concept of heaven itself is dualistic and therefore, illusory.

✓ Attainment of self-realization, which is devoid of all differentiations and resulting pains, can only be attained as a result of flawless, stepwise and steady spiritual processes.

Sometimes, while making efforts to attain self-realization, a seeker may be granted fruits of mundane value while following Vedic path of action due to non-comprehension of the sacred act.

Such fruits may involve extra-sensory experiences. However, in such instances, it is advisable to accept it and keep walking on the spiritual path, without getting attached to those fruits.

✓ Sages and sacred scriptures have unanimously proclaimed that the world is an illusory projection of ignorance (due to *avidya*) and therefore isn't eternal.

✓ A seeker must practice utmost caution, patience and perseverance until this illusory notion of worldliness is erased and the Beyond is realized.

✓ Also, a seeker needs to be consciously aware that mistakes and failures are common in any practice or on any path and the same needs to be rectified, without blaming anyone i.e. others or oneself.

Therefore, self-enquiry (*atma-vichar or atma-vishleshan*) and discrimination (*Vivek*) between real and unreal are the crux of the spiritual practice until one attains self-realization i.e. the Self resolving into the egoless state.

During such practice, over a period of time, harmony is achieved in the elements i.e. earth, water, air, space etc. and apparent duality or distinctions are rooted-out.

The Self and the jiva of worldly life

The universes and their cycles are not eternal but they come and go. However, the Self and the Vedas which proclaim the existence, knowledge and bliss of the Self are both eternal and timeless.

- Though the sacred scriptures preach self-discipline in all worldly matters yet *jiva* indulge in temporary worldly enjoyments by unchecked and indiscriminate use of senses.

- An unbridled mind can never comprehend the Self, just as a dull student can't understand various aspects of taught knowledge.

➤ Even if a jiva has knowledge of matter i.e. triad of gunas or various aspects of body, mind and intellect, such knowledge can't relieve him from bondage.

Pure intellect called 'I' and the constant pursuit of trying to know, understand and comprehend this 'I' through basic question 'Who am I' leads one to self-realization.

➤ Unchecked sensual behaviours lead to agitations in mind and such a state of mind adversely affects the spiritual pursuits of a seeker, just as ripples affect any reflection in water.

➤ For a clearer reflection, water must be pure i.e. clean of impurities and static or stable. Similarly, for self-illumination, a seeker's mind has be clean of worldly impurities and stable i.e. not distracted worldly pleasures.

➤ To remain attached to and pursuing worldly pleasures and aspiring self-realization are contradictory, as the world being an illusion created by mind is 'unreal' and mortal while the 'Self' is 'real' and eternal.

Only those seekers, who don't care at all about the worldly pleasures, are prepared and qualified for their spiritual journey of seeking the 'Self'.

Just as light-houses guide ships to the shore, Shrutis are the guiding-lights for a seeker. And just as high sea-waves as well as storms try to misguide a ship, mundane as well as celestial forces aspire to disturb a seeker in his pursuit of the *Samadhi* state.

To overcome various obstacles in the spiritual path, a seeker must adhere to the Guru's advice and instructions, in letter and spirit.

It is advisable to attain this union with the 'Self' i.e. the *Mahesvara* or the 'Self-realization' in this lifetime itself, else this cycle of rebirth will continue till this union is achieved.

The Self is as It is i.e. devoid of qualities, attributes, adjuncts etc. and is not limited by time-space reference i.e.

The Self transcends the time-space frame of reference and all limitations of forms, thoughts etc.

The Self enlivens the universe including all its animate and inanimate forms through It's own power-stream of consciousness.

Though It appears to embrace and get embraced, It can't be touched by this universe.

Just as 'space' penetrates everything, the Self penetrates everything including the space and yet It is not modified, as does space.

The Self is the repository of consciousness, which illuminates and animates the universe and there is no force that can illumine, animate or know the ultimate Self which illuminates and animates everything else.

Air is termed 'vital' upon entering the body and it appears as if 'vital airs' determine the life in body. However, air gets its vitality from the Self.

A body is rendered dead once the Self withdraws its presence from it and due to this withdrawal of the Self, vital air loses its vitality, leaves the body and merges with the air outside the body.

The Self, which provides motility to various body movements through vital airs i.e. *Prana*, is itself ever unmoving because motion is not the nature of the Self.

The five sense organs, mind and intellect are the driving forces of the body in this world, with mind being the interface between the elemental world and the transcendental Self.

The Self seems to develop or assume an affinity to the vital airs and other elements while discharging power to the mind.

Owing to the apparent affinity, The Self which is ever pure, eternal and illumined, appears to become connected to or interwoven in the inert world and this apparent connection leads to divergent faiths and contradicting philosophies, as this affinity become liable to differing interpretations.

The self, by Its nature is spread throughout everything in the universe and is not different in diverse bodies. Just as same electric current powers a fan, refrigerator, TV and other appliances, the Self powers the entire world.

Though the actors are mortal bodies, yet actions are ascribed to the unmoving Self. When a jiva acquires a body by it's past karma, the embodied Self is thought of as the apparent experiencer of pains or pleasures. However, it lasts only till the demise of the mortal body. The Self is, however, immortal.

Fluctuation and agitations of mind caused by unbridled senses leads to fatigue of mind, which renders one's mind incapable of entering the Heart, the seat of the Self.

Total abidance in the Self is possible only after eradication of ignorance and stopping the mental traffic by taming the senses, thereby having a thoughtless state.

A lot of folklore and misguided beliefs patronise and endorse indiscriminate sense-indulgence throughout life and then attempting to escape the karmic repercussions by remembering Isvara at the fag end of life. A sincere seeker is never fooled by such falsehoods.

~ Om Namah Shivay ~

11. Spiritual path

Bhagwan Shiva proclaimed that spiritual path is a long and arduous journey for every seeker and one goes through many joyous and frustrating stages on this journey.

There is no denying the fact that every joyous experience motivates a seeker to keep moving forward on his spiritual pursuit. However, whenever a seeker experiences obstacles or a seeming failure on his spiritual path, being a jiva with body, mind and intellect and their related tendencies; it is natural for him to feel bitter, exasperated and impassioned.

Such states of mind confuse him between worldly attractions and spiritual ideals. The fear of failure might redraw him towards worldly enticements and pleasures.

It happens so because the spiritual journey is an uncharted path whereas the worldly life is known to the individual jiva; and it is natural to revert to a known territory instead of moving forward on an unknown and uncharted path.

However, a careful analysis of the situation and self-examination (*atma-vichar*), careful discrimination between real and unreal (*Vivek*) with a dispassionate and detached mind will reveal the illusion of worldly enticements as well as supreme inner glory and blissfulness of his spiritual ideal i.e. the Brahman.

Even during daily temple visit, mundane daily worship or daily ritualistic worship such as sacred fire-ceremony *(homa)*, one must have Brahman as the ideal as well as the goal.

Perseverance on spiritual path through a firm determination, unquestioned faith and devotion to achieve the Brahman acts as the protective shield of the seeker in times of seeming failure or against the enticements of worldly objects and sensual pleasures.

A seeker always ought to eulogise, glorify and celebrate his ideal, the Brahman and fully recognise that the ultimate aim of all knowledge, faiths and religions is attainment of That, the Brahman.

Intense desire for attainment of the Brahman and final liberation plays the key role in a seeker's spiritual journey till his mind has subsided by ending all its distracting thoughts.

A seeker must acknowledge and accept that all the distracting thoughts of his mind are nothing but dormant or latent tendencies accumulated over innumerable lives that were lived in ignorance.

By carefully comparing materialistic worldly life and spiritual path, he can ascertain the momentary pleasures of worldly actions and the lasting bliss of spiritual journey.

Role of Mind

Our mind is a repository of past experiences, samskaras, unfulfilled desires and ever increasing desires due to fulfilment of lot of desires. These act as obstacles or blockade for new blissful experiences and therefore, one needs to cleanse one's mind of these obstacles through *yoga, pranayama, atma-vichar* (self-enquiry), meditation and contemplation.

Though it is painful in the beginning, yet gradual cleaning of one's mind of its latencies accumulated over innumerable lives, certainly yields invaluable fruits.

A pure mind experiences results as promised in the Vedas without even knowing the reasons of the same or source of their authority.

Sometimes a seeker experiences illumination as a result of fulfilment of studying and adhering to the tenets of the sacred texts in their previous lives.

Sage Suka (son of Ved Vyas) was an outstanding example of such studies and adherence as he experienced the Brahman owing to his accomplishments in past lives.

Even the scriptures have celebrated his life's achievements inspiring *Vairagya* (renunciation) from worldly life and love for the ideal, Brahman among the seekers.

(Sri Ramana Maharishi, who attained atma-vidya at the age of seventeen is an example of the same.)

The authority and supremacy of the Vedas is unquestioned and final and they are followed and explained by the *Smrities*.

Both Vedas and *Smrities* are the beacon lights, guides or lodestars in a seeker's inner journey knowledge.

A body is essential as the basis for a seeker and he must use the knowledge of scriptures to progress towards the 'Self'.

Without getting enticed or distracted by the worldly objects and pleasures thereof, a firm conviction in the 'glory of the Self' transcending all materialistic pleasures is the assurance of liberation *(moksha)*.

Ignorance in the mind of jiva of the ever-shining nature of the Self is a reason of not knowing the Self and it results in running after fleeting and momentary worldly pleasures.

Removal of this ignorance *(avidya)* is the only means to know and comprehend the ever present Self.

When consciousness (which powers a jiva's body, mind and intellect) is conditioned by jiva's body, then it is commonly termed as *'Atman'* or soul.

By constantly reflecting on its source Brahman, Atman becomes progressively illumined and learns to ascertain light of the Brahman within and without and attains unity with the Brahman.

A seeker's progress in the spiritual journey is reflected in his non-attachment to worldly objects and not getting enticed or distracted by worldly pleasures. It is to be remembered that 'subject' is one, pure and eternal while 'objects' are myriad, impure, causing pleasure and pain and transient or momentary.

Therefore, constant vigilance and conscious alertness is required by a seeker to not fall for the worldly objects.

Downfall from scriptural austerities

If one suffers downfall from scriptural austerities on his spiritual path, one need not despair because such downfall doesn't spoil the achievements and such spiritual seekers start their spiritual journey in another incarnation from wherever they left it in this incarnation.

The gradual progression on the spiritual path brings increased responsibilities and a seeker must carry on his practices with greater joy and zeal.

Guru's grace helps erase the world impressions from one's mind completely and thereby, the Self is revealed in all its glory and liberation is achieved.

Even the occasional distractions and disturbances of mind, veiling the Self, subside gradually and the state of Samadhi becomes nature of the seeker.

At the later stage of spiritual progression, involving subsidence of Atman in the eternal Brahman, one might have anomalous and unusual experiences.

In these confusing situations, the sacred texts help a seeker through proper explanations. Then, one need not look back and finally the *Jnana* (knowledge) dawns on him, erasing ignorance completely.

At this final stage, craving for pleasures might surface owing to either the body's sickness or worldly distractions. After all, till body is alive, it will try to use its senses, mind and intellect causing these cravings.

Such craving is completely and strictly prohibited for a seeker. It can only be done by constantly training and reinforcing the mind with renunciation and non-attachment, to avoid any chances of retrogression.

Self-Realization liberates a jiva from rebirth cycle. However, if one attains Self-realization while there is still time for the body to dissolve itself, one must keep performing mundane actions required for it to maintain itself as well as those ordained by Sastra, but without any sense of 'doer-ship' and constantly being established in remembrance of Lord Shiva and one's Self.

Finally, Bhagwan Shiva ends his Instructions by saying –

These unparalleled aphorisms given as instructions by ME from the Sastras are both enlightening for the spiritual aspirants / seekers and inspiring for those who are still entangled in the samsara (transmigratory existence) in this world of objects.

This world is only a shadow of My universal abode of transcendental bliss – The SELF.

~ Om Namah Shivay ~

Epilogue

The Almighty Shiva has succinctly described the creation of the universe, the Brahman, the Consciousness, the Self, apparent duality and the reasons thereof and the role and import of sacred texts, and Self-realization and obstacles thereof.

However, every wise and true seeker needs to remember that only reading sacred texts to show-off or reading sacred texts without honest intent isn't enough.

Therefore, it is important to resist the temptation of outwardly loud, exhibitive and pompous reading of sacred texts or acts depicting the same without a deep desire, sincere intent and devotion to reach the Almighty.

Lord Shiva is the embodiment of inner and outer peace, humility and simplicity and unostentatious love. So, He needs to be constantly remembered and worshipped with noiseless prayer, quite joy, sincere affection, supreme peace and total humility.

This way only one shall be able to see Him losing to oneself in all fullness.

~ Om Namah Shivay ~

About Authors

Anshu Chaudhary is a spiritual and creative person, wherein she is passionate about reading, writing and painting. She is an experienced human dynamics professional and entrepreneur with extensive humanities education through her Masters in Psychology, MBA in HRD, PG Diploma in Human Rights and Diploma in Urdu Language.

Raj Bhambu has donned various hats i.e. of being an Indian Army Officer, a Banker, and a Corporate Leader in MNCs, an Entrepreneur and an Author.

Raj and Anshu have published three Self-Help books prior to this latest one. They are titled:

1. Work-Life Mantras

2. You @ Your Best

3. And worked happily ever after

www.ingramcontent.com/pod-product-compliance
Lightning Source LLC
Chambersburg PA
CBHW022027150726
47990CB00002B/849